C0-BJH-108

Tackling Anxiety

How to Regain Your Peace of Mind

By Ernest S. Schmidt, LCSW

Copyright Information

Copyright © 2009 by Ernest Schmidt of Palo Alto Therapy, All Rights Reserved.

Except as permitted under the United States Copyright Act of 1976, no part of this publication may be reproduced or distributed in any form or by any means, or stored in a database or retrieval system, without the prior written permission of the publisher.

If you become aware of unauthorized copies of any of our books in either electronic or hardcopy form, we would appreciate learning the details. Please send a letter to our physical address or e-mail to schmidt@paloaltotherapy.com.

ISBN 978-0-557-19279-3

ABOUT THE AUTHOR

Through my personal and professional life, I've learned many intricate details about anxiety and its characteristics. Since 1996 I have been dedicated to helping people work past problems in order to reach happier, more fulfilled lives. My education includes a bachelor's degree in psychology from the University of the Pacific, a master's degree from UC Berkeley, and a certification in cognitive therapy through the Academy of Cognitive Therapy.

When I am not running my psychotherapy practice, Palo Alto Therapy, you can find me working as a tenured faculty member of Foothill College in Los Altos Hills, where I offer personal counseling, train and supervise new therapists, and teach anxiety-ridden students the basics of self-help strategies, stress management, and emotional wellness. Before stepping into my current positions, I served as a lead therapist with Santa Clara County Mental Health, where I supervised a team of specialists who provided therapy to young adults and their families.

My therapy and teaching methods are direct, down-to-earth, and personable. Through writing and distributing this book, I hope to expand on my overall mission, which is to help my clients achieve their goals without long-term counseling. I believe that change can be made within a relatively short period of time, with focused therapy and an honest effort from the client.

TABLE OF CONTENTS

INTRODUCTION

My goal in writing this book is to give you an easy-to-use guide that can help you change your struggles with anxiety. By using clear and simple writing, I have transformed the information I've learned as a therapist into language that is easy to understand. Anxiety, though very treatable, is often misunderstood and not properly managed. Most of the general public is totally unaware of how therapists or psychologists help their clients. Through the process of learning this fundamental information, you can improve your life and begin to tackle your anxiety. By learning the most effective methods used in treating anxiety, not only will you feel better but you will be able to live without the roadblocks connected with this difficult emotion.

This introductory guide can provide you with hope and a different outlook on anxiety. This new perspective will also allow you to see that anxiety does not have to be a huge, lifelong burden that must go untreated. Instead, with the proper understanding and your will to work at it, you'll find that your anxiety is quite manageable.

I've Been There Too

In many instances, I myself have benefited greatly from the information I'm presenting in these pages. I've worked on my own anxiety, such as social anxiety, public speaking anxiety, and finally, in my role as a therapist and teacher, performance anxiety. This knowledge has not only helped me personally, but as a therapist I have used it to help hundreds of people who struggle with anxiety to find peace of mind.

Although coping with anxiety never seems simple, if you follow the suggestions I offer and put in a good, solid effort, improving your situation is very possible. However, reading this book by itself, without any sort of attempt to practice the techniques in your day-to-day life, will likely leave you disappointed. How realistic is it to expect transformation in your life without making any changes?

The tips in this ebook require some work. I am not talking about hard manual labor, but you will need to complete some written exercises and put these ideas into practice. You'll see that if you do this, you will not only be able to understand anxiety better, but you will learn how to greatly reduce it as well. Isn't a life with less anxiety worth a little work?

" When I look back on all these worries I remember the story of the old man who said on his deathbed that he had a lot of trouble in his life, most of which had never happened. "

Winston Churchill

1. WHAT IS ANXIETY?

Anxiety Is an Emotion

Although this is simple to say and sounds almost too basic, it is easy to forget that anxiety—a feeling of apprehension, uneasiness, or fear—is an emotion. This point is important to remember, since we all experience all kinds of emotions to some degree, at one time or another. However, you may feel anxious and not even realize it; instead you may feel tension in your muscles, snap at people around you, get angry, or pull back from social events, to name a few ways anxiety may affect you. The most important thing to understand is that, like sadness, hurt, anger, shame, regret, or guilt, anxiety is really just a normal human emotion. These are all things you feel, and they are all very, very normal.

Everyone Experiences It

Everyone has some degree of anxiety. I repeat, "Everyone has **some** degree of anxiety" in his or her life. Whether the person is you, a family member or friend, a neighbor or colleague, one of the best ways to deal with anxiety is through understanding it. In most situations, I do not see anxiety as a mental illness or a disorder. Rather, I see anxiety as something all of us will eventually deal with, sooner or later, in one form or another. Throughout the course of your lifetime, you will encounter different situations that will cause anxiety in yourself or your loved ones; that's just a fact of life. However, what you do with the anxiety once you are aware of it is what truly sets the tone for what happens in your day-to-day life.

Having the ability to understand anxiety is at least half, if not more than half, of the battle in learning how to reduce it. When you truly are aware of anxiety and its characteristics, you will feel less ashamed, learn to fear it less, and experience reduced anxiety as a result.

What Does Anxiety Feel Like?

For some of you, anxiety is extremely physical:

- Racing heart
- Feelings of nervousness inside your body
- Trembling
- Sweating
- Pacing or tapping your fingers
- Stomach discomfort or feelings of butterflies
- Nausea or even diarrhea

For others, anxiety is less physical and more hidden. Often you may be totally unaware (or in denial) that you even experience this emotion. I can't count how many times I have heard things like "I don't have any anxiety; I am just lucky that way," or "I  don't have anxiety; I just worry sometimes," or what my dad recently told me that made me laugh, "I don't have anxiety; I am just concerned." (Do you see the humor in this?)

Sometimes people deny that they experience anxiety to avoid appearing weak or different in some way, but I also believe many people just don't understand what anxiety is. In these types of people, anxiety can look quite different from the physical reactions mentioned earlier and can include:

- Irritability
- Distractibility or lack of focus
- Feeling stressed or uneasy
- Feeling worried, concerned, nervous, or afraid

- Drug or alcohol use or abuse
- Other repetitive behaviors such as laughing a lot, continual talking, checking things over and over, etc.
- Feeling on edge or extremely uncomfortable, but being unsure why

These symptoms can all be the result of anxiety, whether you know it or not! Anxiety can be incredibly sneaky.

There have been times in my own personal life when I've been unaware of how anxiety was affecting me. When I was contemplating a job that included teaching and frequent public presentations, I was quick to say that such work did not interest me. I really believed that teaching was just something that I did not want to do, that I preferred to do something else purely out of choice. But when I had time to think about this, I realized that my anxiety was what I preferred not to deal with. It wasn't the act of teaching that turned me off; it was the public speaking, because of my anxiety. Once the anxiety was dealt with, I found that teaching was actually a passion of mine. How sad would it have been if I had kept believing my own lies and continued to let anxiety fool me? I have seen anxiety do the same thing to my clients countless times, and often they ask, "How do I know if it's my anxiety that is stopping me from doing such and such or if I really just don't like it?" This is a difficult question to answer, but maybe if you are asking this question you already know the answer!

What Makes You Feel Anxious?

Anxiety is synonymous with fear, nervousness, worry, concern, or being on edge—these are all emotions that are classified as anxiety. Although you may think of these emotions as less severe than anxiety, they are really all the same emotion. For instance, going out in public and meeting new friends may cause you to worry. Other times, speaking in front of a group of people might trigger you to be nervous. (Public speaking is known to be the

number one greatest fear; for some, this fear is even greater than the fear of death!) But there are other less obvious things that can also make you feel anxious or worried: job interviews, dating, planning an event such as a wedding or party, watching your children grow up or go off to college, or even exercising (you may fear looking silly or too overweight, etc.).

The first day of school always made me feel pretty anxious. Sometimes if I have to do something I'm not used to doing, like registering for college classes or going to the DMV, I feel anxious about not knowing the "rules" or general protocol. Or I will feel anxious if I've never done something before, like traveling to a new country or seeing a client with a problem that I am not very familiar with, etc. These are just some of the things that make me nervous. Try to think of what makes you nervous, worried, or anxious.

Anxiety and Performance Level

To best handle the emotion of anxiety, you not only need to increase your awareness of it as mentioned before, but you also need to change your negative view of it. You can do this by thinking about how vital anxiety can be when it comes to your level of performance or how you function in various aspects of your life such as work, school, etc. I realize this may be difficult to get your head around, but in some ways anxiety can actually be beneficial. Anxiety is not necessarily the painful, evil emotion that it has come to be known as. Think of it in terms of what I call the "Performance Graph" or the "Stress Anxiety Diagram." See the diagram below.

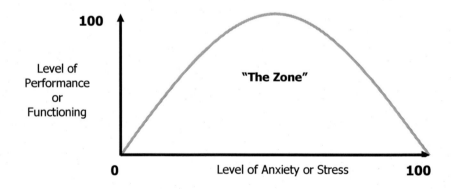

According to this diagram, low anxiety equals low performance. Let's say you're looking at anxiety and performance on a scale from 0 to 100, with 100 being high anxiety or high performance and 0 being low anxiety or low performance. If your anxiety is very low—at or near 0—I believe your level of performance will also be very low. Here's why: If you don't feel any fear or any sort of pressure—no real stress at all—I believe you won't really be at the top of your game. But as you get more nervous, you become more prepared in a way. Although I am slightly changing the definition of anxiety here from "nervous" to "being prepared for something," this slight twist in thinking can help you in dealing with anxiety.

Try to think of how anxiety has helped you in the past. Has it made you study harder for a big exam? Have you done extra research for a critical work presentation because of worry? Anxiety can really heighten your attention, focus, and determination, but only to a certain degree. Take a look at how the curve on the anxiety diagram goes up, and then rounds out and comes down the other side. Your top performance is at the very top of that arc, which I, as well as others before me, call "The Zone."

Think of athletes and how they feel before big games. They will almost always feel some pressure or have the experience of getting "psyched up." Maybe you have heard of the "pre-game jitters." All of these experiences can be defined as forms of anxiety, but if you were  to ask top athletes to give this up, you would have quite a battle! Without this pre-game anxiety or excitement, they wouldn't perform up to their potential. Even some of the top athletes such as Michael Jordan, Martina Navratilova, or Mary Lou Retten would attest to this: In situations like these, you want to have a certain amount of anxiety or a certain nervousness to help you be well prepared for what you're about to do.

It's Healthy to Be in the Zone

Having said that, I must add that too much anxiety can lead to problems. When you push yourself too far or if you feel too much pressure or anxiety, your performance will drop. Look at what happens to performance at the far right of the diagram: As anxiety approaches 100, performance approaches 0. Why? You become distracted! You may start to physically shake. You find you can't concentrate as well. You might even have stomach pains or feel some of the other physical reactions that were previously discussed. Maybe your memory is negatively affected when you get so nervous; you may even stumble over your words as you start speaking faster; perhaps you stutter. All of these effects can negatively impact your performance.

This performance graph not only shows that anxiety is normal, but also reinforces the idea that you are not trying to get rid of your anxiety. Given this concept, you almost never want your anxiety to be at zero. If a client were to ask me for help with his or her anxiety, I'd say, "Look, you're not trying to go from 90 to 0 on the diagram; you're trying to go from 90 to maybe 60 or 40." When you see anxiety from this new perspective, you will experience an immediate reduction in anxiety. You no longer feel the pressure of trying to totally eliminate your anxiety. Imagine trying to never again feel sad, happy, angry, or other normal emotions. Talk about anxiety!

2   WHAT TYPE OF ANXIETY DO YOU HAVE?

No discussion about anxiety would be complete without examining the different types or classifications of anxiety problems.

Phobias/Social and Performance Anxiety

Phobia just means you're intensely afraid of something specific, or afraid of doing a particular thing, such as public speaking. Fear of public speaking is the most common phobia. Another pretty common phobia is social phobia or social anxiety, which can be defined as being afraid of or nervous about interacting with people and/or going to social events. Common symptoms of social anxiety include:

- Anxiety and self-consciousness in everyday social situations
- Fear of being watched and judged negatively by others
- Being embarrassed or humiliated by one's own actions
- Physical symptoms like blushing, sweating, trembling, nausea, and difficulty talking

Other phobias can be fear of blood, germs, spiders, etc. Now, I don't necessarily think of these anxiety problems as disorders; instead I view them on a continuum from mild to severe. In most cases, for a problem to be classified as a disorder, it must be causing significant distress in the important areas of your life, such as work, relationships, and/or ability to experience pleasure.

For example, with social anxiety, it may just be shyness or a bit of anxiety in social situations, but when you have such intense shyness that you are unable to leave your home or make any sort of social contact, then you would likely have a disorder or phobia. Regardless of the technical language, these problems or disorders are all under the umbrella of anxiety. This is an important point, since they will all be treated in similar ways, with similar methods.

Performance anxiety appears to be less talked about in the psychological manuals, since it is not considered a disorder in the traditional sense. However, this type of anxiety is very common. You may have experienced this when you have had to perform in a sporting event, musical competition, or possibly a talent show. Performance anxiety can also rear its ugly head during important work presentations, interviews, or anytime you are trying to do something well and are feeling the pressure. You may not have connected this feeling with the word "anxiety," but it is all the same emotion.

Panic Attacks

A panic attack, although horribly distressing for most people, is really just an intense feeling of anxiety at a given moment: intense, immediate feelings of anxiety and the feeling of total discomfort.

If you've felt like you're going crazy, that if your anxiety worsens you're going to go crazy, you're going to die, you're going to lose your mind—or maybe you've felt like you'll have a heart attack or you are scared of passing out—and this is all associated with extreme physical reactions such as heart racing, sweating, flushed face, nausea, dizziness, all in a matter of between 5 and 30 minutes, then you've likely experienced a panic attack.

Although these fears are quite real to you at the time and therefore trigger the anxiety and physical reactions, none of these fears actually comes true when you have panic attacks. In reality, these attacks are pretty easily treated if you are motivated and want to learn more about them. I'll discuss that in greater detail later in this book.

Obsessive-Compulsive Anxiety

The obsessive-compulsive type of anxiety sounds complicated and unfortunately is not accurately displayed in the popular media. In reality, "obsessive" refers to your repetitive thinking about one particular thing or a number of things. And "compulsive" pertains to your behavior; you do something, some unique action, and you do this something over and over again. So "obsessive" is thinking about something over and over, and "compulsive" is doing something over and over.

For example, let's say your obsessive-compulsive trigger is safety. So you continuously worry about your family's safety or your individual safety; that's your obsessive thinking. Your compulsive behavior or action may be to repeatedly check the locks on your doors or to check the windows to prevent someone dangerous from entering your home. Every time your worry about this danger resurfaces, you reassure yourself by double-checking that the house is locked and safe, not only once or twice but multiple times.

To the outside person this "compulsive" or repetitive behavior seems extreme or bizarre, but once you understand the anxiety or fear behind it, it makes perfect sense. It's helpful to understand that there is an anxiety problem at the root of Obsessive Compulsive Disorder (OCD) and that if you struggle with it, you're not crazy, but rather you are highly anxious. This type of anxiety can be quite difficult to change since the person gets some relief (and therefore reinforcement) from doing the compulsive behavior and may have a hard time stopping it. Even with this complication, obsessive-compulsive anxiety is very treatable with the right tools, education, and guidance.

General Anxiety

And then there's the mixed bag of "general anxiety," which is a combination of the common day-to-day worries like:

- Worries about global crises

- Worries about money

- Worries about relationships

- Worries about health or loved ones, etc.

Of course, there are other types of anxiety disorders, such as Post Traumatic Stress Disorder (PTSD), which I won't be discussing at this time. I mention this so you will, at least, understand that this diagnosis is also an anxiety disorder that can be well treated.

3. BEHIND THE SCENES OF ANXIETY

When thinking about anxiety, it's important to note how **YOU** perceive it! This is the most important piece to understand, because what you *think* greatly influences how you're going to *feel*.

Double-edged Sword

For instance, when you have anxiety you tend to have thoughts of danger, of being threatened, or you feel vulnerable, you fear being hurt, and you may fear being socially rejected, humiliated, or embarrassed. Thus, an important theme of anxiety is that you <u>overestimate</u> the consequences that are likely to occur. For instance, if you're at a social event you may fear you're going to be totally  humiliated in front of everyone. Or that you will make such a big fool of yourself that no one will invite you to another party. This is what I mean by overestimating consequences.

The second part of this, sort of the double whammy, is that you <u>underestimate</u> your ability to cope with what you fear will happen. For example, you may fear that the people at the party are going to totally reject you; that's where you overestimate what's really going to happen. But, in the process, you also <u>underestimate</u> how you will handle the rejection if it does happen. You may be afraid that you would have to run out from the party, or that you would never get over the embarrassment (die from embarrassment), or the shame would be so bad that you would just have to stay home from that day forward, and so on.

I call it the double-edged sword of anxiety: You overestimate the feared consequences and underestimate your ability to cope with those consequences. So when you're working on managing your anxiety, not only do you need to be aware that this is happening, but you also need to target both of these tendencies.

What If ...?

Anxiety also tends to be "future oriented," so you make a lot of predictions. You predict things are going to go bad, and you may express your predictions with a lot of "what if" statements. Like "What if the plane crashes?" "What if I look strange in front of people?" "What if I act funny?" "What if I lose my job?" "What if I fail my English test?" "What if I have cancer?"

When you feel anxious, you may also see images of some sort in your head. You're not crazy; in fact, this is something many of us do if we are truly in tune with how we think about things. Many times, we have images in our mind that reflect what we're thinking. When you are feeling anxiety, you may occasionally have an image of a plane crashing or an image of someone laughing at you when you're making a speech, depending on what's making you nervous at the time.

More about Panic: The Snowball Effect

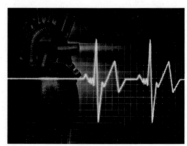

When you struggle with anxiety, you can sometimes experience one or more panic attacks. As stated before, this really is just extreme anxiety that's all packed into 5 to 30 minutes. "Panic" is a mixture of emotional and physical symptoms. The "emotional" is the anxiety, the fear, the dread, the discomfort. The "physical" symptoms are the rapid heartbeat, the sweating, the shaking, the dizziness, the pain in the chest, the hot flashes, the chills, and being a bit disoriented. The difficulty with panic attacks is that they are formed as part of a vicious cycle.

For example, you may feel a little anxious for any number of reasons, which may increase your heart rate, much like everyone's heart rate goes up and down throughout the day. But if you struggle with panic attacks, you may start thinking and worrying about the increase of your heart rate and think, "Oh, my gosh, I'm going to have a heart attack." Or, "Oh, my gosh. What's happening? Something's wrong!" And the snowball grows.

This type of thinking will then trigger a greater physical response such as an even greater increase in your heart rate, or perhaps your breathing rate will increase, which will then automatically increase your heart rate. The oxygen in your system will then increase, which will then escalate many of the other physical symptoms! This is the vicious cycle of panic attacks: The more physical symptoms you have, the more you start interpreting those symptoms incorrectly, and then your thoughts and physical reactions play off one another. You think, "Oh, my gosh, I'm going to have a heart attack," or, "Oh, my gosh, I'm going to die or something really bad is going to happen," then you start feeling more and more anxious, and poof, you are now in a full-blown panic attack!

Let me give an example of what a panic attack can look like in a more subtle form. Planning our wedding was a very stressful experience for both my wife and me, but particularly for my wife. She had heightened anxiety throughout this process, which at times formed into a panic-type response. At the time, neither of us recognized what was happening or what it was since the problem appeared more physical. For the longest time she believed it was a food allergy. Whenever it hit her, she would experience stomach cramps and feel very nervous, her face would get bright red, her heart would race, she would get the chills, she would even become nauseated, throw up, and one time she ended up in the emergency room thinking she'd had a severe allergic reaction. After many visits to doctors, talking with me about the effects of anxiety, and seeing that these problems all went away once the wedding planning was done, my wife finally realized this was all created by her anxiety about the big event. A nice, but painful, example of how sneaky anxiety and specifically panic attacks can be.

Although there are different forms of anxiety, understanding the similar themes of this emotion will greatly assist you in fighting back. Having this background knowledge about anxiety will also make it less intimidating as you apply the skills in the following pages.

"Although the world is full of suffering, it is full also of the overcoming of it."

Helen Keller

4.   Overcoming Anxiety

Now let's talk about some of the ways of overcoming anxiety. There is a lot to this, and although it can seem rather simple when you read about it, it can be quite difficult when you try to do these things yourself. Please remember that this is only an introduction to the various methods to work on anxiety and is not comprehensive. Even though you will likely need more details once you fully commit to working on your anxiety, this overview will give you the confidence and peace of mind that it can be done. I am hopeful that by seeing what anxiety treatment looks like you will be less afraid of it, more willing to actually try it, and therefore will benefit from it!

The Fuel of the Fire

One of the first things I like to do when working on anxiety is to reduce the shame that is associated with it. When people feel anxious, extreme or otherwise, they tend to feel ashamed or guilty because of it … like anxiety is some sort of personal weakness or that it's abnormal. This can become another vicious cycle related to anxiety—not only are you feeling nervous, but you begin to feel ashamed because of that nervousness, and then you feel abnormal as a result. You may even think subconsciously to yourself, "Gosh, I'm really abnormal;  someone's going to spot this." This type of thinking then adds fuel to the fire and actually makes you more anxious.

So imagine if you were sort of nervous in a social setting. You may have some low-level nervousness mixed with some excitement and apprehension since you're not sure what to expect. But if you start thinking about your anxiety and how awful it is and how everyone is going to spot it and you're going to be totally ashamed and people are going to make fun of you for it, you will then begin to feel more nervous because of that shame. That's the vicious cycle I'm talking about.

The shame that stems from these negative thoughts actually makes you feel worse than the emotion itself. If you try to suppress your anxiety because you think you shouldn't be feeling these emotions, you're only compounding the situation. In fact, the shame you attach to feelings of anxiety makes working through those feelings much worse than if you just dealt with the root of the problem head-on. Believe it or not, sometimes the majority of the pain we feel is actually *because* of the shame, not the underlying emotion itself.

If, as you're getting ready for that party, you could realize that your anxiety is nothing to be ashamed of, you would be able to say to yourself, "Hey, everybody has this; it's not a big deal." This mindset would allow you to eventually get over this initial anxiety, and you would be able to enjoy the party. I realize this sounds too easy, but that is the purpose of really understanding anxiety, so that you are more equipped to deal with it effectively.

Social Support: Extinguish the Shame!

Social support is an important part of getting treatment, or help, for anxiety. Whether you want to call it treatment or not, social support is just you sharing with those around you that you experience anxiety. By doing so, you'll find that most people—family, friends, colleagues, neighbors down the street, celebrities, politicians, and others from all walks of life—have some degree of anxiety and generally will not think less of you for it. When you are able to share about your anxiety and experience this reaction, your shame becomes much less of an issue. Since anxiety is one of those things that we tend to judge ourselves harshly for, we don't typically talk much about it. We also expect that everyone else will judge us the same way we judge ourselves, so the shame lives on. If you really want to make progress with your anxiety, sharing that you feel anxious is a powerful step that's worth taking. Not only do you get to hear many people around you admit to their own anxiety, but you also get to see with your own eyes that you are rarely judged as you expected, and the shame is thereby extinguished.

Many times, I've seen how confronting the shame associated with anxiety can make a huge difference in people's lives. In my class at a local community college, I teach students about emotions, wellness, and various ways of coping. Anxiety and stress are a major focus of the class. I require many self-help-type exercises for homework and encourage the students to share their results with one another. Through this process, many students go through an amazing transformation from being reserved and restrained about their personal problems to feeling almost excited to share. Their shame vanishes when they have the courage to share it with others. Not only do they feel better in just expressing themselves, but their fellow students begin to chime in about how they've felt that way or how "messed up" their own emotions are. That is an example of social support at its best. This class doesn't totally eliminate anxiety, but for many students this clearing of the shame and guilt associated with their feelings seems to be all they need to perform better and improve their peace of mind.

I recently saw further evidence of the value of social support when I ran a group for people struggling with anxiety. In the group meetings, I introduced many tools that I believe can make a big impact on the intensity of anxiety. I helped the group understand what anxiety is and showed them how to use a thought record and begin changing the way they think, among many other techniques. Even with all the other tools I offered them, many group members told me that the simple act of expressing their fears and talking openly about their anxious feelings was a big help in reducing their anxiety and the shame associated with it. In one particular meeting, an individual discussed a situation that was making him anxious. The other group members quickly identified both with him and his feelings. When this individual saw that not only did the group not reject him when he revealed his feelings but actually became more accepting of him, his anxiety level began to decrease. The group became closer when they accepted one another's perceived flaws or limitations and saw that they were not the only ones who felt this way. In future meetings, the members were visibly more relaxed and became more social and laughed more together—largely because they had shared their feelings in a supportive setting. This is a powerful example of how reducing shame and guilt is one way to help in getting a handle on anxiety.

Breathe in, Breathe Out

Another way of reducing anxiety or better managing it is called "relaxation training." One form of this is called "controlled breathing." This is where you focus on your breath by trying to breathe in very deeply and very slowly. Try breathing maybe 8 to 10 breaths a minute … really, really slowly. Just take deep breaths and slowly exhale. You also want to try to get the oxygen and the breath as deep into your lungs as you can. One way to practice getting oxygen really deep into your lungs and creating a deep relaxation feeling is to put one hand on your stomach and one hand on your chest. Then take in a breath, inhaling deeply so that the hand on your stomach moves the most and the hand on your chest mostly stays still. In this way, you are breathing mostly in your abdomen and less in your chest. This process tends to turn on the relaxation response and helps you avoid heightening your panic or anxiety. Try this now for a few minutes.

Controlled breathing is a very nice tool to relax you and slow down your nervous system when you're anxious. Focusing on your breathing in this way not only turns on the relaxation response but also helps as a bit of distraction. It's impossible to be relaxed and nervous at the same time. So by training yourself to breathe correctly you will actually take over that "stress response" or "anxiety response" and turn on the "relaxation response."

In Your Mind's Eye

You can also do relaxation training using what's called "guided meditation" or "guided visualization" (see Visualization Exercise in the Resources Section). You close your eyes, practice the deep breathing, and then picture a place in your mind. You can call this your "safe place" or "relaxation place." Although you may find this corny, as some of my students do, I think you'll find it useful once you actually practice it.

Think of a place that you've been to—a vacation spot, an exotic beach, a place in your house; it can be in your bedroom or the garage that you like to relax in—any place where you have felt very relaxed and at peace. Picture that place in your mind. Try to imagine every single aspect of that situation. Try to use every sense: What colors do you see? What sounds do you hear? What smells do you smell? Does it feel like anything? Do you feel the salty mist in the air? Do you feel the cold wind on your face? Do you feel the hot sun on your legs? That kind of thing. As you close your eyes and visualize this, make sure to also use the deep breathing. If you practice this visualization technique enough, you will find that within three to five minutes you can get yourself into a very relaxed state.

For example, when I use visualization I pick a lake that I go to every summer. I have a small sailboat there that I take out on the lake, and whenever I am feeling a bit stressed or anxious before a presentation I close my eyes, picture my relaxation place, and practice my breathing. No one will even know I am doing this. I can do this before I enter the room. I just close my eyes for maybe two minutes; I picture the lake and see the mountains. I'm looking at the lake, feeling the sun; I can hear the water on the shore and some birds overhead. All these imagined sights, sounds, and feelings can put me into a really nice relaxation place and quickly turn on my relaxation response. The power of our minds is a wonderful thing.

If you doubt the effect of this type of visualization, all you have to do is think of a stressful place such as the dentist's chair and take stock of what you begin to feel as you picture it. I know for me, I begin to tense my muscles and I can almost hear the drill and experience the smells that are connected with my prior visits. I don't have any proof other than my own internal reactions, but I am sure by doing this I am beginning to turn on my stress or anxiety response.

Although breathing and visualization exercises are easy to implement and somewhat helpful in managing anxiety (that's why I included them here), they are not nearly as powerful as the skills that I discuss in the rest of this e-book.

Changing the Way You Think

One of the key components to tackling anxiety is changing the way you think. Altering your thought patterns can greatly reduce your anxiety, or even lead to completely overcoming it. Think of this as shifting the way you think or changing your perspective. Remember, the goal is not to totally eliminate anxiety. Trying to get rid of all anxiety is not a normal thing to do. It's like trying to get rid of all sadness or anger. If you succeeded, you would be an emotionless robot. That's not your goal. You can feel a lot better just by taking on this new perspective of not trying to completely rid yourself of anxiety.

Reduce the Pressure

The harder you push away anxiety, the stronger it comes back, putting much more pressure on you. So one thing you want to do is reduce the pressure. You can do this by not trying to make your anxiety go away. You want to try to accept it to some degree; accept that it is normal to feel anxiety. If this makes sense to you and you understand anxiety really is a normal emotion, then you have already succeeded in changing your thinking.

This shift in perspective can provide amazing results. Picture the benefits of responding to future anxiety like this: "I am feeling anxiety right now and it's making me uncomfortable, but it's a very normal emotion. I am feeling highly anxious, but it's not dangerous, it's just an emotion and I can handle feeling it!" This type of response would stop the vicious anxiety cycle in its tracks. Changing the way you think about anxiety will not only reduce the pressure you feel but will also cause a reduction in your overall anxiety.

Thought Record

A "thought record" is another effective method to change the way you think about anxiety. (See the sample thought record on page 35 and  the Complete Thought Record in the Resources Section.) This is a method to record your thoughts when you are feeling anxious or, put another way, to record all the thoughts that make you anxious. The first step in changing the way you think is simply being more in tune with your thoughts. This awareness is the perspective that I talk a lot about. The more you are aware of what you are thinking—and the more you're aware that your thinking directly influences your anxiety levels—the more you're able to really change your level of anxiety, and in some cases totally overcome it! Not eliminate it, but overcome it. To "overcome" anxiety means that not only will your anxiety be lessened but you will also learn to function very well even with anxiety, because anxiety is a normal emotion, a normal human emotion. I will keep repeating this until you get it.

To complete a thought record, you first record a few small details about the situation you were in when you started feeling anxious. Secondly, you record the emotions you were feeling and rate them from 1% to 100% in terms of intensity. Next you write down all the thoughts you had when you were anxious, or you can pick a situation that you are currently in and record those thoughts. Although this may seem unnecessary, it is crucial! Don't skip the "writing down" portion of this process, as there is something about putting these thoughts on paper that helps your perspective and eventually your anxiety levels. You may find it difficult to capture these anxious thoughts. For many, this is the hardest part of completing a thought record, but if you use the tip questions I have provided, you should be able to do quite well.

 THOUGHT EXERCISE:

What are you thinking right now, in this moment? Maybe you are thinking, "Wow, this is really boring. I wish I was doing something else" or "This makes perfect sense. I really get this" or "What is for dinner tonight? I am hungry." These are all thoughts, but not necessarily the thoughts that make you anxious. Understanding what your thoughts are and then being able to identify them is a skill that may take some practice, especially when it comes to the thoughts that make you anxious.

Once you have flushed out all of the anxious thoughts or the thoughts that you believe are behind your anxiety, the next step is to look them over closely. When we are plagued by anxiety or any other intense emotion, we tend to feel whatever we are thinking simultaneously, without any filter or perspective. If I am anxious about speaking to a group of people and I have the thought "I will make a fool of myself," I will feel scared, anxious, and ashamed almost immediately. In these kinds of situations, we don't take the time to see what is happening and we get overtaken by our anxiety.

By practicing with thought records, not only do you learn to critique what you are thinking in the moment, but you also begin to delay and then reduce the emotional response of anxiety. Thought records force you to examine the emotionally powerful lies that you frequently tell yourself. Yes, that's right, lies! Just thinking something doesn't make it true. Thoughts do not equal facts. Time and time again, therapists have found that when people are feeling highly anxious their thoughts are mostly untrue or distorted in some way. Once you spot these untruths or distortions, the power behind these thoughts is greatly diminished, and you are left with much less anxiety! Imagine what would happen to your anxiety if every time you told yourself a lie—"I am going to fail this test" or "He will turn down my proposal"—you just didn't believe it. Sometimes just the act of writing down your thoughts and seeing them can start unraveling your anxiety. However, this is only the first step, and often you may need to do more work in order to spot the lies or distortions in your thinking.

What Does "Distorted" in "Distorted Thinking" Mean Anyway?

"Distorted" means inaccurate, irrational, not quite right, false, not completely true, or that there is an error of some sort. When it comes to distorted thinking, all of these definitions will work. Distortions in thinking take many forms:

Mind Reading: **Adapted from the best selling book Feeling Good by David Burns**

You automatically assume you know what others are thinking or feeling. Even if you have good reasons to believe you are correct, you are often wrong. "She's angry with me," "They think I'm boring," "He's disappointed in me."

Fortune Telling:

You predict the future in mostly negative ways. "I am going to fail the test tomorrow," "The audience will be bored with my material," "I will never get promoted," etc. Very often this type of fortune telling causes unnecessary worry and anxiety. Last time I checked, no one could predict the future with 100% certainty.

"Should" Statements:

You tell yourself that you should or shouldn't do things. These statements carry heavy judgment as well as unnecessary shame or guilt. "I shouldn't be so nervous," "I shouldn't have called the boss," "I should be stronger and more patient," etc. When I run into these thoughts, I like to ask, "Who says you should or shouldn't?" Another way to help with these "should" statements is to think in terms of "would like" or "would prefer." Such as, "I would prefer not to be so anxious right now, but I am." By slightly rephrasing these thoughts, you can greatly reduce the negative impact on your mood or anxiety. Remember you are not trying to eliminate anxiety completely.

Labeling:

You negatively label yourself through broad generalizations—"I am a nervous wreck, a loser, a jerk, a failure"—but you leave out the crucial specifics and don't realistically evaluate your current situation—"I am tight due to my nervousness and my voice is quivering, but I am not a nervous wreck."

Negative Filter:

Have you ever heard the saying "She sees the world through rose-colored glasses?" Well, a negative filter is just the opposite, more like mud-colored glasses. This means that you tend to view the world in a negative way and you pay for it with heightened anxiety or other uncomfortable emotions. This perspective keeps you focused on the negatives while you ignore the positives. If your filter is really strong, you are convinced that the positives don't even exist. "I never do anything right," "My parents never complimented me," "I feel nervous all the time."

Overgeneralizing:

This distortion mostly defines itself. You make sweeping statements based on one or two events. You oversimplify or take a broad view that is not well supported by the circumstances. "He is always rude to me," "Traveling is always difficult," "All employers expect perfection and are unforgiving."

Magnification:

You blow things out of proportion or magnify them beyond what is factual. You give too much importance to one thing or situation, and this causes unnecessary emotional distress. "I am the biggest jerk in the world," "I will die of embarrassment," "I am having a nervous breakdown."

Catastrophizing:

This means you tend to think in terms of catastrophes or disasters. "Because I forgot to put out the napkins, the whole party is ruined," "My career is over since I blanked out during my presentation." Upsetting events can be difficult to deal with, but they are usually not catastrophic. When you exaggerate the effects, you torture yourself with unnecessary anxiety.

All or Nothing or Black and White:

You see things all one way or another—either black or white—with no middle ground. "I am unsuccessful" or "I am a bad wife/husband." The world typically does not work this way. Usually things occur on a range or continuum. Often things are neither black nor white, but a shade of gray. Are you really unsuccessful at everything at all times, or just some things some of the time?

Emotional Reasoning:

You make assumptions based on how you feel; you ignore the facts, but are excessively tuned into your feelings. For instance, "I feel worried, therefore I am unsafe" or "I feel guilty, therefore I did something wrong" or "I feel discouraged, so I must be hopeless." Although your emotions may be telling you something important, often they are way off base and are not supported by the facts.

One way to feel better is to first identify the thoughts that are causing your anxiety and then check to see if any of these thoughts have errors or distortions in them, as listed above. For instance, when I feel anxious, sometimes I think people will *see* that I am anxious and *think* that I am weak. This thought causes me sadness, shame, and excessive anxiety. If I look for distortions or errors in this thought, I will see that there are many: fortune telling, mind reading, and labeling, to name just a few. Do I really know that people can see my anxiety or that they will always think badly about me because I appear anxious? I am also labeling myself as weak, but is the mere fact that I feel anxious enough reason to conclude that I am a weak human being or somehow less than someone who isn't feeling anxious?

By using thought records to help me find these distortions, I show myself that my upsetting thoughts are not entirely true, and this realization results in less sadness, shame, and anxiety. You may be thinking that this method is too simple to make any difference (a perfect example of fortune telling!), but in reality it can be a powerful tool to help you feel better.

In case you still have doubts, consider the case of a young man I once worked with who was struggling with obsessive-compulsive disorder. One of this young man's particular problems was his excessive guilt and anxiety regarding the passing of his mother. Among other things that he seemed to find helpful, he particularly liked using the thought record to identify his thoughts. We found his most distressing thought behind his anxiety and guilt was "I am responsible for my mother's death." Uncovering and talking about this was extremely painful for him, evident by his tearfulness, but it also proved to be highly rewarding. By writing and being able to talk about this distressing thought, he could finally look at it from a different perspective. He ran the thought through the distortions test and found, with some struggle, that it fell into the all-or-nothing category; he had been telling himself that he was *completely* responsible for his mother's death, when in fact that was far from true.

The young man was convinced that his mother would have lived hours or even days longer if only he had been by her bedside. A part of this conviction remained even after our work together, but once he'd done the distortions test, the son saw more clearly that he was not *completely* responsible for his mother's death. At first he was feeling close to 95% guilt and anxiety over his original thought, but once he saw through this he was able to drastically reduce his emotional response. We agreed that it was acceptable for him to feel some level of guilt and anxiety over not having been at his mother's side; however, feeling this at the 95% level was excessive. Although this view could be argued further or even looked at negatively, for this young man it was a major breakthrough. His guilt and anxiety around the memory of his mother practically vanished, largely due to the use of the thought record and list of common distortions.

Spend some time reviewing the list of common distorted thought patterns and see if you can spot any errors in your own thinking. Do any of these patterns sound familiar? Identifying these distortions in your thinking will help you in completing the thought record and in managing your anxiety. The final step is to record an alternative thought for each thought that originally made you anxious (see the sample thought record below).

Sample Thought Record

Situation

I was preparing for giving a presentation at work on Thursday at 6:30 p.m.

Emotions and Intensity 1-100%

Anxious 85%   **Worried 90%**   **Ashamed 75%**

Thoughts	Distortions Found	Alternative Thoughts
I will bore the audience and lose credibility.	Fortune Telling, Magnification	Some of the audience may get bored, but it's unlikely that one presentation will make or break my career.
I will freeze up and look like a fool.	Fortune Telling, Labeling, Magnification	It's possible I will be tense, but I have never frozen in the past. If I look really nervous and stutter, I might be embarrassed, but I won't be a fool. Some people may judge me for this, but many others will relate to my being nervous.
I shouldn't be nervous; I am so weak.	Should Statements, Negative Filter, All or Nothing	I would be happier if I was more relaxed, but I guess I need more practice. Public speaking is nerve-wracking for most people. I am anxious, but this does not mean I am weak; it means I am human and I care about my performance.

By spotting and removing the distortions, you can develop an alternative way of viewing the situation. This gives you practice in responding to your anxious thoughts by coming up with thoughts that are much more accurate, balanced, and less anxiety provoking. Although it does take effort at first, this skill will become second nature in a matter of weeks and is one of the most powerful weapons in tackling anxiety.

Changing Your Behavior

The last thing I'll discuss regarding overcoming anxiety is also the most crucial step: changing your behavior. "Behavior," a term commonly used by professionals in the field of psychology, is what you do or how you act. When I spoke earlier about the obsessive-compulsive type of anxiety, I explained that when you have those fears of safety you act by checking the locks or windows. That behavior at first reduces anxiety, but in the long run it actually causes anxiety to keep coming back, or in therapy language, it "maintains your anxiety." The more you check the locks and see your anxiety drop as a result, the more you convince yourself that checking is the only way to reduce your anxiety. This reinforces you to check again and again, becoming another vicious cycle that can be difficult to stop.

Everyone with high anxiety will avoid, to some degree, the things that make them anxious. As in the example above, checking the locks is a way for people with obsessive-compulsive anxiety to avoid their anxiety. So the term "avoidance" is a very, very bad word when it comes to anxiety. If you want to truly tackle your anxiety, you will need to stop avoiding!

Avoidance

This symptom, termed "avoidance," is often the most destructive of all and generally the least recognized by individuals who suffer from anxiety. Some turn down quality job offers that include an element of public speaking, whereas others consistently pass up social engagements.

Other ways that you may practice avoidance are as follows:

- Online gaming, web surfing, or TV watching
- Alcohol and drugs
- Overeating
- Sleeping
- Not calling friends
- Not saying hi, avoiding people, or not making eye contact
- Skipping school/work presentations

Much of this avoidance is out of your awareness, and you will start to find your daily activities and your enjoyment in life becoming more and more restricted. There are several ways to overcome anxiety, but unless avoidance is addressed, it is difficult to make significant and long-lasting progress.

Exposure

"Exposure," or exposing yourself to anxiety, is the exact opposite of avoidance. I want you to understand that the more you try to run from your anxiety and avoid things that make you nervous, the more anxiety chases you, and the more you have to actually work to get a handle on your anxiety. The behavior part of anxiety treatment, or overcoming anxiety, is learning to change your behavior by actually seeking out anxiety—not avoiding it but actually pursuing it! That can really change your relationship with anxiety and consequently greatly reduce the power it has over you.

I realize that facing the things that you fear will cause intense anxiety itself, but that is why it's important to work on your thoughts and fears first. By doing this you can prove to the rational part of your brain that it is a good idea to do the exposure or to face your fear. Of course this depends on what you are afraid of. If you fear picking a fight with three huge wrestlers, then you should keep your anxiety right where it is, but if you fear making a presentation in front of people, well now we are talking. Yes, you can reduce anxiety just by doing the mental exercises of challenging your thoughts as described earlier, but you won't see total success until you see for yourself that your fears do not come true. This is one of the reasons why exposure is the most powerful weapon against anxiety.

Imaginary Exposure

Low-level but effective exposure can be as simple as visualizing your worst fear or what makes you the most anxious. One 34-year-old student I worked with had intense anxiety whenever she had to perform a medical procedure in front of her supervisor. She practiced very hard and meticulously studied the material to try to prevent making any mistakes. The nights before her big exams, she even started trying to imagine herself performing flawlessly in the hopes that this positive visualization would benefit her the next day. But no matter how well she knew the material, or how many times she imagined herself doing a great job, her nervousness kept disrupting her performance. When we worked together, we went almost straight to exposure. Her exposure was to imagine herself doing a terrible job in front of the most critical supervisor in the program. She was instructed to seek out her anxiety and try to inflame it. (Although this may seem like torture, it's actually the best medicine; see page 39-40 for more explanation.) Rather than imagine the best-case scenario as she was trying to do prior to working with me, her homework was to imagine the worst possible situation. Once she got comfortable with this intense level of anxiety and realized she could handle the worst outcome possible, her performance anxiety greatly diminished. Her next exam was nowhere near what she had put herself through in her mind, and she was able to perform at a much greater level, with only a moderate amount of anxiety.

My Exposure Experience

When it came to my public speaking anxiety, I did a lot of work on my anxious thoughts (with paper and pencil), but the real results came when I finally taught my first class in front of 30-plus college students. This was the perfect exposure since it was regular (twice a week), it lasted long enough for my anxiety to rise and fall (an hour and 20 minutes), and it went on for a good amount of time (three months). Although this exposure produced high levels of personal anxiety for the first part of the quarter, as time went on, I felt more and more at ease. The work I had put in on challenging my thoughts was very helpful (it gave me the courage to even try teaching), but nothing was better than facing my anxiety in real life and seeing that my thoughts really were untrue. Or as I always say, the proof is in the pudding.

Ending the Conflict

Once you turn and face anxiety, the struggle stops, the conflict ends; you show yourself that you do not have to fear anxiety, and you also prove to yourself that anxiety cannot hurt you. Exposure is really the final nail in the coffin when it comes to managing this often-distressing
emotion. Once you fully understand anxiety and challenge the thoughts that produce it, you then need to "expose" yourself to it. With proper exposure, you learn the most important aspect of anxiety: that whatever you feared was not as bad as you thought, and no matter how things turned out, you are able to cope! The following tables will help explain this concept.

Avoidance

You choose to leave the situation or run from the anxiety "Avoidance"

But … anxiety comes right back next time!

2

4

1

3

Anxiety starts going up!

Anxiety drops (in the short term …)

- Don't feed your anxiety

    - The more you avoid it, the more you believe you can't cope with it or with the consequences of it

    - It feels good to avoid anxiety, so you reinforce yourself for continuing this pattern

Exposure

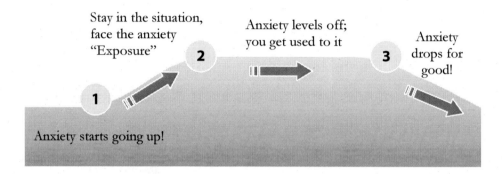

Stay in the situation, face the anxiety "Exposure"

2

Anxiety levels off; you get used to it

3

Anxiety drops for good!

1

Anxiety starts going up!

Why??

- Learning occurs:

  - You see that nothing extremely bad happens

  - You see that you can cope with whatever happens

  - You adjust to your anxiety and see that your anxiety doesn't keep increasing

What Else Happens with Exposure?

- It reduces your conflict with anxiety

- It changes your relationship with anxiety

- **No more** struggle!

By truly learning these lessons over and over through exposure, you finally break the spell of anxiety as you realize the more you fight anxiety, the more it holds on. I know this may sound like a fairy tale, but after witnessing this scenario many times over and personally experiencing the effects, I am convinced.

CONCLUSION

Understanding anxiety is key in managing it, but the most important thing is that you actually implement the techniques I've presented to tackle your anxiety. Perhaps you've struggled with anxiety for years without being fully aware of how it affects you. Perhaps you've passed up promising job opportunities because you fear public speaking, or maybe you've become socially isolated because you're extremely nervous about meeting new people. If so, or if you've felt other long-term effects of anxiety in your life, you'll be glad to know that managing your anxiety is not as complicated or as impossible as you might think. The information and techniques presented in this book can help you live a more relaxed and healthier life—if you absorb the information and put the techniques into practice. I hope that reading this book has inspired you to take some steps towards regaining control of your life. It is also my hope that through this introduction you now see and truly understand that anxiety is very treatable and that you will take full advantage of the help that is available.

FREQUENTLY ASKED QUESTIONS

1. What's the difference between anxiety and an anxiety disorder?

Nothing really, except the intensity and the impact on your life. If you are significantly impacted by anxiety, you likely have what is called an anxiety disorder. To me, it's all the same thing, just at different levels. (See page 9 for more discussion of this.)

2. How can I tell the difference between anxiety and worry?

You can't, because to me they're the same thing. Worry, fear, anxiety, nervousness—these are all the same things. These are normal human emotions and are nothing to be ashamed of. Some of us are more bothered by our anxiety than others, and I guess some of us need more assistance in this area for whatever reason, but anxiety is just an emotion that you need to first understand and then learn to manage. There are some simple ways to reduce anxiety, and you don't need to spend years in therapy to do this.

3. How do you control your anxiety without anxiety meds when it gets the best of you?

First you stop trying to control it. By trying to control anxiety you actually make it worse. This may sound too much like "therapist talk," but you need to change your relationship with anxiety. Most of us run and hide as fast as we can from anxiety. We are afraid of it. We are ashamed of what people will think of us if we look anxious. One very simple way of controlling your anxiety is to turn and face your fear. This can mean literally doing the thing that you fear the most over and over again until you find that your anxiety drops, which it will. Some people may not want to start with this technique called "exposure," but it does work and it is the fastest way to see results. It's like pulling off a band aid quickly and intensely versus slowly and carefully. Exposure takes quite a bit of courage, but in the end many prefer it.

The other way to change your relationship with anxiety is to face your fears by writing them down on paper. Actually think of what you are afraid of when you are feeling anxious and PUT IT ON PAPER. I know this step may seem unnecessary since you will say that you already know what you are thinking, but there is something about writing your fears down and seeing them on paper that will help you. At first it may be difficult to find out what is making you afraid, but try to think, "What am I afraid will happen when I speak in front of people?" Maybe I will faint, or I will lose my words, or I will mumble, or I will look anxious and they will see that I am anxious, or I will not impress them enough, or they will ask questions, etc., etc., etc. Get your own anxious thoughts on paper and see what happens. This is actually called cognitive therapy, or looking at your thoughts to see how they affect your emotions and behavior or actions. We think anxious thoughts, we feel anxious, we avoid or intensely tremble during the presentation.

Once you have your list, you can try to see if there are any thoughts on it that are irrational or not very accurate. You can try to spot what we call distortions or errors in your thinking: "Am I exaggerating here?" "Am I ignoring all the positives and focusing on the negatives?" "Am I reading the minds of people without truly knowing what they think?" "Am I fortune telling and predicting the future without my handy dandy crystal ball?" Sometimes spotting these errors also helps in your work to reduce the power they have over you.

Another technique is to then write down what you would do next if your fears actually came true. (See Coping with Feared Outcomes in the Resources Section.) YES, do this as well. For each fear write exactly what would happen next and how you would handle it and see what that looks like.

There are other techniques like this that have tremendous power to change your relationship with anxiety, but this is a good place to start. Sometimes you can do this alone with a good self-help book and high motivation. Others like to have someone, such as a cognitive therapist, to help them along or coach them on how to use the techniques.

RESOURCES

1. Complete Thought Record

This is one of the most powerful tools for anxiety reduction. I would also say it's the bread and butter or the foundation of most cognitive therapy. See page 29 for an in-depth explanation of how and why to use this exceptional tool.

2. Visualization Exercise

This is a good exercise to do if you would like to develop a personal visualization exercise for relaxation or anxiety management. It is mostly self-explanatory, so just read the directions and create your own script.

3. Coping with Feared Outcomes

This form is to help you deal with the double-edged-sword aspect of anxiety, the part of you that believes you are unable to cope with bad outcomes. Recording your worst fears, or what you believe would be the worst-case scenario in a particular situation, and thinking about and writing down how you would handle this can greatly empower you. This form not only makes you face your fears by thinking about them, but it helps you come up with rational responses and reactions to difficult situations. By doing all of this, you can greatly reduce your anxiety. See FAQ #3 for more information.

4. Anxiety Tracking Tool

Use this form to monitor your anxiety on a daily basis. This will help you become more aware of your anxiety and its characteristics. You will see any patterns to your anxiety that may help you better focus your efforts. The comment section can be used to gather your anxious thoughts or experiences on the actual day that you experienced them. Just tracking your anxiety can be a great, low-intensity way to begin working on it.

Complete Thought Record

Name _____ **Date** _____

Situation

Very brief explanation. Who were you with? What were you doing? Where were you? What time and day was it?

_____

Emotions and Intensity 1-100%

Use one-word answers such as depressed 80%, nervous 30%, angry 40%, guilty 70%, sad 90%, etc.

_____   _____   _____

Thoughts	Alternative Thoughts
If someone were to draw a cartoon of you at the moment you were upset, what would be in the thought bubble above your head? What were you thinking about when you were upset? How did you view the situation? What was on your mind that may have caused the above emotions? Examples: "She meant to insult me." "I acted like a total idiot." "This is impossible."	How else could this situation be interpreted? Could someone else see things differently? How? Are your thoughts exaggerated or unrealistic in any way? How? Is there a more balanced way of viewing this situation? How? What thoughts could you have that might be more helpful to you?
Find Distortions ➡	
Find Distortions ➡	
Find Distortions ➡	
Find Distortions ➡	
Find Distortions ➡	
Find Distortions ➡	

Visualization Exercise

1. **Read this once all the way through without doing anything. Then read it again and follow the instructions.**

   Get as comfortable as you can, and close your eyes. Take three, slow, deep breaths and begin to focus on your breathing. Now I want you to think about a place you have been to before that is peaceful, safe, and relaxing. Sometimes people picture the beach, a certain room in their house, a vacation spot, or any <u>specific</u> place that is calming and relaxing for them. Take a moment and picture this relaxing place....

   When you have this place in your mind, look around in your mind's eye and see what you notice. Try to use all of your senses. What colors do you see there? Notice whether there is a certain temperature or sensation against your skin ... Is it warm or cool? Notice whether you can hear any sounds ... Is there one specific sound or are there many? Look around and pay attention to all the colors, sounds, and sensations. Take a few moments to enjoy the experience of being in your peaceful, relaxing place.

   Soon, I want you to come back from your safe place knowing that you can always return to it anytime you close your eyes and take three deep breaths. When you feel you have really pictured this place and felt yourself there, go on to step 2.

2. **Get a pen and paper or use a computer to write/type what you have imagined. Remember these key points:**

   - Include every detail
   - Use the present tense as if you are there right now
   - Describe this place using all five senses
   - Record all the feelings that you feel when you are there

3. **Once you have completed this, try imagining this place 3-5 times a week for 10-15 minutes at a time. Practice deep breathing during the process as well. Feel free to also use the anxiety tracking tool to help you decide if this exercise is an effective tool for you.**

Feared OutComes Worksheet

Feared Outcomes or Worst-Case Scenario (Record what you fear will happen. What results are you most afraid of?)		**Realistic Coping Responses** (Record what you would do if your fears were to come true. Write down the steps you would take to address or manage the feared outcomes. If this outcome were to happen to a friend, how would you tell them to handle it? Use specifics.)
	➡	
	➡	
	➡	
	➡	
	➡	
	➡	
	➡	
	➡	
	➡	
	➡	

Anxiety Tracking Tool

Name _____

Start Date _____

Instructions: At the same time each evening, mentally review the intensity of your anxiety/nervousness and then circle the number that best represents your level for the day.

Anxiety Scale 1-10	Sunday	Monday	Tuesday	Wednes-day	Thursday	Friday	Saturday
Calm	1	1	1	1	1	1	1
	2	2	2	2	2	2	2
	3	3	3	3	3	3	3
So-so	4	4	4	4	4	4	4
	5	5	5	5	5	5	5
	6	6	6	6	6	6	6
	7	7	7	7	7	7	7
Very Anxious	8	8	8	8	8	8	8
	9	9	9	9	9	9	9
	10	10	10	10	10	10	10

Comments/Observations:

Sunday _____

Monday _____

Tuesday _____

Wednesday _____

Thursday _____

Friday _____

Saturday _____

RECOMMENDED READING

Davis, Martha, & McKay, Matthew. *The Relaxation & Stress Reduction Workbook* (Paperback). New Harbinger Publications; 6th edition (May 3, 2008). 371 pages.

Greenberger, Dennis, & Padesky, Christine. *Mind Over Mood.* (Paperback). The Guilford Press; 1st edition (March 15, 1995). 243 pages.

Burns, David. D. *Feeling Good.* Harper. Reprint edition (October 1, 1999) 736 pages.

Lyubomirsky, Sonja. *The How of Happiness.* Penguin (Non-Classics); Reprint edition (December 30, 2008). 384 pages.

Hyman, Bruce M., PhD, & Pedrick, Cherry, RN. *OCD Workbook.* New Harbinger Publications; 2nd edition (August 2005), 237 pages.